Sensational Science Projects with Simple Machines

Robert Gardner

Enslow Elementary

an imprint of

Enslow Publishers, Inc.

40 Industrial Road	PO Box 38
Box 398	Aldershot
Berkeley Heights, NJ 07922	Hants GU12 6BP
USA	UK

http://www.enslow.com

Enslow Elementary, an imprint of Enslow Publishers, Inc.

Enslow Elementary® is a registered trademark of Enslow Publishers, Inc.

Library of Congress Cataloging-in-Publication Data

Gardner, Robert, 1929–
    Sensational science projects with simple machines / Robert Gardner.
      p. cm. — (Fantastic physical science experiments)
    Includes bibliographical references and index.
    ISBN-10: 0-7660-2585-3
    1. Simple machines—Juvenile literature. I. Title. II. Series
    TJ147.G38 2006
    621.8'078—dc22   2005008974

ISBN-13: 978-0-7660-2585-1

Printed in the United States of America

10 9 8 7 6 5 4

Illustration credits: Tom LaBaff

Cover illustration: Tom LaBaff

Contents

(Experiments with a 🏅 symbol feature **Ideas for Your Science Fair**.)

Introduction

How can a 50-pound boy lift a 200-pound man? You can find out by doing experiments with simple machines. Doing experiments will help you understand how machines make work easier. This book will show you how to build and experiment with each of the six types of simple machines—lever, wheel and axle, inclined plane, wedge, screw, and pulley.

Entering a Science Fair

Some experiments in this book (those marked with a 🎖 symbol) have ideas for science fair projects. However, judges at science fairs like experiments that are creative, so do not simply copy an experiment from this book. Expand on one of the ideas suggested, or develop a project of your own. Choose something you really like and want to know more about. It will be more interesting to you. And it can lead to your own experiment that you plan and carry out.

Before entering a science fair, read one or more of the books listed under Further Reading. They will give you helpful hints and lots of useful information about science fairs.

Safety First

To do experiments safely, always follow these rules:

❶ Do experiments under adult supervision.

❷ Read all instructions carefully. If you have questions, check with the adult.

❸ Be serious when experimenting. Fooling around can be dangerous to you and to others.

❹ Keep the area where you work clean and organized. When you have finished, clean up and put all of your materials away.

1. Force, Friction, Distance,

To understand simple machines, you have to first understand force, friction, distance, and work.

A force is a push or a pull.

❶ Have **an adult** place a concrete block in a child's wagon. Put a force on the wagon by pulling it. The wagon will move. Forces make things move. Push on the wagon. Again, it will move.

Things you will need:
✔ an adult
✔ concrete block or similar weight
✔ child's wagon
✔ ball
✔ bathroom scale
✔ concrete or blacktop surface
✔ thin rope or clothesline about 6 feet long
✔ yardstick
✔ 5-pound bag of sugar

❷ Earth pulls on everything. Earth's pull is called gravity. Drop a ball. It falls because gravity pulls it downward.

❸ Earth pulls on you. Stand on a bathroom scale. The scale measures Earth's force (pull) on you. That force is your weight. How big is Earth's pull on you?

gravity
(a force)

Let's Look at Friction

Friction, like weight, is a force. And friction can be measured.

❶ Ask **the adult** to put the concrete block on a concrete or blacktop surface.

❷ Put a piece of rope or clothesline about 6 feet long through an opening in the concrete block. Tie the ends of the rope together to make a loop.

❸ Put the free side of the loop around a bathroom scale. Holding the scale, use it to pull on the concrete block.

The block won't move until you pull with a certain force. The force that resists your pull is friction. Friction always acts against motion.

4 How hard do you have to pull before the block just barely moves? That force is friction acting against the block. How much friction is there? (Read the scale.)

5 Measure the force of friction on an upright wagon loaded with the concrete block. (Have **the adult** load the wagon.) You can wrap the rope around the handle and use the scale to pull on the wagon. Is friction against the wagon less than friction against the concrete block by itself?

scale

rope

concrete
block

To measure distance, all you need is a yardstick.

1 To measure distance, ask an adult to help you measure your height. That is the distance from the floor to the top of your head when you stand. How tall are you?

2 To measure work, you have to measure two things—distance and force. Why? Because in science, work equals force times distance.

$$\textbf{work} = \textbf{force} \times \textbf{distance}$$

Work is easy to measure. Lift a 5-pound bag of sugar 1 foot high. You did 5 foot-pounds of work.

$$\textbf{work} = \textbf{5 pounds} \times \textbf{1 foot}$$
$$= \textbf{5 foot-pounds}$$

How can you do twice as much work?*

* Answer: Lift the 5-pound bag 2 feet, or lift a 10-pound bag 1 foot.
  Are there other ways to do twice as much work?

2. First-Class Levers

A lever is any bar or rod, such as a seesaw, that can be used to lift things. A fulcrum is a support for the lever. A 1-inch-by-6-inch board about 5 feet long can be your lever. The lever must rest on a fulcrum. A 1-inch-by-1-inch board about 1 foot long can be the fulcrum.

Let's Begin!

Things you will need:
- ✔ 1-inch x 6-inch board about 5 feet long
- ✔ 1-inch x 1-inch board about 1 foot long
- ✔ a friend
- ✔ brick

❶ Place the fulcrum (smaller board) under the lever about 18 inches from one end (see drawing).

❷ Have a friend sit on the lever's shorter side.

❸ Lift your friend by pushing down on the longer side of the lever.

❹ Apply your downward force (push) at position 1, then 2, and then 3 (see drawing). At which place do you have to apply the least force to lift your friend? At which position do you have to push hardest to lift your friend? Are there places where you cannot lift your friend no matter how hard you push?

❺ With the fulcrum at the same place, replace your friend with a brick. The brick will probably not raise the long side of the lever. Can you explain why?

❻ What can you do so that the brick will raise the other side of the lever?

1

2

3

fulcrum

18 in.

First-Class Levers:

There are three classes of levers. You made a first-class lever. It makes work easier. The load (a friend) was on one side. To lift your friend, you pushed down on the other side of the lever. You did work. You applied a force through a distance.

Your work was easiest when you pushed down farthest from the fulcrum, at position 1. (Look at the drawing on page 13.) Think about distance first. The distance your friend moved up was small. The distance you pushed down (from the top of the lever to the ground) was larger.

Now, think about force. You pushed down with a small force at position 1. Your friend's weight was a large force.

Work, which is force times distance, was about equal on both sides of the lever.

$$\text{F} \times \text{D} \approx^{*} \text{F} \times \text{D}$$

| your small push | large distance you pushed | friend's large weight | small distance friend moved |

* ≈ means "about equal." Your work is always a bit more. A little extra work is needed to overcome friction between the lever and the fulcrum.

An Explanation

Closer to the fulcrum (positions 2 and 3), you had to push harder. You needed bigger forces to make up for pushing shorter distances. Pushing on the fulcrum, no matter how hard, cannot turn the lever.

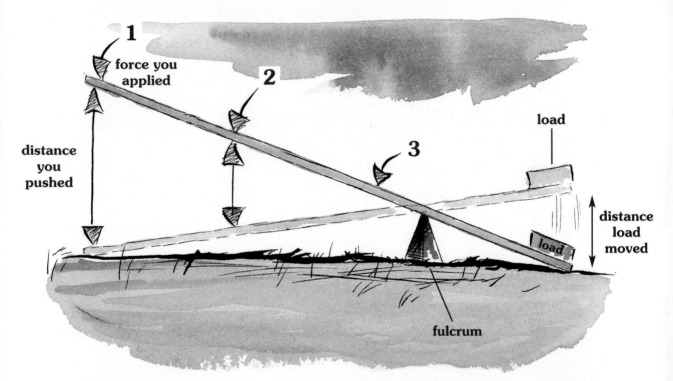

Ideas for Your Science Fair

★ Show that a seesaw is a lever.
★ Where can you find levers in your home and in other places?

3. Second-Class Levers

A second-class lever makes work easier, but it differs from a first-class lever. In a second-class lever, the load is between the fulcrum and the lifting force (see drawing). Both are on the same side of the fulcrum.

Let's Begin!

1 Put the lever on the fulcrum.

2 Put the brick on the long side of the lever at position 3.

3 Raise the brick by lifting at positions 1, 2, and 3. Where is it easiest to lift the brick? Where is it hardest?

4 Put the brick at positions 1 and 2. For each position, lift at the end of the lever's long side. At which position is it easiest to lift the brick? At which position is it hardest to lift it?

5 Have **an adult** put a concrete block in a wheelbarrow (a second-class lever). Put the block at position 1L, 2L, or 3L.

6 Lift at the end of the wheelbarrow's handles. Predict at which position (1L, 2L, or 3L) it will be easiest to lift the block. At which position is it hardest to lift it?

7 Put the load at position 3L. If you lift the handles at positions 1, 2, and 3, where will lifting be easiest and hardest? Try it. Were your predictions correct?

Second-Class Levers:

Second-class levers also make work easier. By lifting with a small force at position 1, you could move a large force (the brick's weight). The key is, you lifted a long distance to raise the brick a short distance. When you lifted closer to the fulcrum (positions 2 and 3), you had to use bigger forces. But you lifted shorter distances. In every case, the work (force times distance) you did was about the same as the work done on the load.

$$F \times D \approx F \times D$$

| **your small force** | **large distance you lifted** | | **brick's large weight** | **small distance brick moved** |

An Explanation

What about the wheelbarrow? Lifting was easiest when your force moved a long distance (position 1) while the load (concrete block) moved a short distance (position 1L). Your hands moved farthest when you lifted at the end of the handles (position 1). The load moved the shortest distance when it was closest to the fulcrum (position 1L). As with all levers, the work you did in each position was about equal to the work done on the block and wheelbarrow.

distance your hands moved

distance load moved

3   2   1

4. Third-Class Levers

Brooms and shovels are third-class levers. Like second-class levers, both the load and your force are on the same side of the fulcrum. In third-class levers, though, the lifting force is between the fulcrum and the load (see drawing).

Let's Begin!

1 Place a brick (load) on the blade of a shovel.

Things you will need:
- ✔ brick
- ✔ shovel
- ✔ broom
- ✔ concrete or blacktop surface

2 Put your right hand on the end of the handle. Your right hand is the fulcrum for this lever.

3 Use your left hand at positions 1, 2, and 3 to lift the load. At which position is it easiest to lift the load? At which position is it hardest?

4 Lift the brick with your hand. How does the force needed to lift the brick by hand compare with the force needed to lift it with the shovel? Does a third-class lever make work easier or harder than a second-class lever?

5 Place the brick on a concrete or blacktop surface. Put your right hand (fulcrum) near the end of a broom handle. Predict at which position of your left hand— 1, 2, or 3—it will be easiest to move the load. At which position will it be hardest? Try it. Were your predictions correct?

Third-Class Levers:

In one way, third-class levers are like second-class levers. The load and the force moving it are on the same side of the fulcrum. But the levers differ. A third-class lever requires more force to move a load.

Think about the shovel. The force you used to move the load was greater than the load's weight. Why? Because the load was farther from the fulcrum than your force. Therefore, the load moved farther than your force (see the drawing on page 21). With this lever, you exerted a big force in order to move the smaller load a big distance.

$$\textbf{F} \times \text{D} \approx \text{F} \times \textbf{D}$$

| your **big** force | **small distance** your hand moves | **smaller weight** of load (brick) | **big** distance load moves |

Again, the work you do and the work done on the load are about equal. Why are you willing to use a big force? When shoveling or sweeping dirt, you want to move the dirt much farther than you move your hand.

With a third-class lever, to make your force smallest, put your lifting hand farthest from the fulcrum (position 3). But you will probably prefer position 2 so that you can move the dirt farther with each scoop.

An Explanation

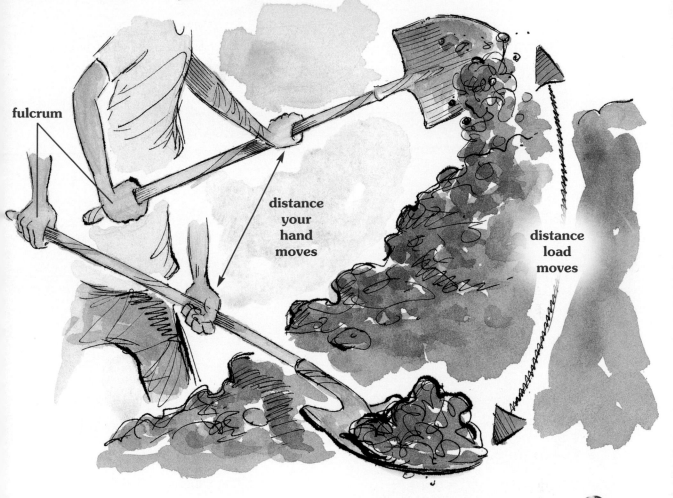

fulcrum

distance your hand moves

distance load moves

Ideas for Your Science Fair

★ Build a model to show that the human forearm is a third-class lever.

★ Collect some different tools. Can you find tools that are each class of lever?

5. The Wheel and Axle

The wheel and axle is a simple machine. It makes work easier.

Let's Begin!

Things you will need:
- ✔ an adult
- ✔ corrugated cardboard
- ✔ pencil compass
- ✔ ruler
- ✔ sharp knife or shears
- ✔ pencil
- ✔ bolt (at least 3 inches long) with a round head
- ✔ 2 washers and 2 nuts that fit bolt
- ✔ string
- ✔ plastic pail
- ✔ measuring cup
- ✔ water
- ✔ 2 tables or 2 chairs

❶ Find a sheet of corrugated cardboard. With a compass, draw a circle about 25 cm (10 in) in diameter on the cardboard.

❷ **Ask an adult** to cut out the circle using a sharp knife or shears. The cardboard circle will be your wheel.

❸ Use a pencil to make a hole through the center of the wheel.

❹ Place a nut and washer on a long bolt (at least 3 inches long) with a round head. Push the bolt through the hole in the cardboard. The bolt will be cardboard

wheel

washer

nut

string

wheel

axle

table or back
of chair

string

your axle. Fasten it to the cardboard with
the other washer and nut, as shown.

5 Knot a string around the axle. Wrap the
string around the axle several times.
It should not slip when you pull on it.

6 Tie the other end of the string to a plastic
pail. Add a cup of water to the pail.

7 Place the ends of the axle on two tables or
the backs of two chairs.

8 Raise the pail (load) by turning the axle.
Then raise it by turning the wheel.
Why is it much easier to raise the load
by turning the wheel?

pail
(load)

The Wheel and Axle:

A wheel and axle, like a first-class lever, makes work easier. One turn of the wheel lifts the load only a short distance. Your pull on the wheel (**F**) was much smaller than the weight of the pail (**F**). But your force (your hand) moved a large distance, **D** (all the way around the wheel), while the pail moved a small distance (**D**) for each turn of the wheel.

$$\text{F} \times \text{D} \approx \text{F} \times \text{D}$$

| **your small force on wheel** | **large distance your force moved** | **large weight of pail** | **small distance pail moved** |

You traded a small force (pulling the wheel) for a large distance. The work you did on the wheel was about the same as the work done on the load (pail).

Lifting the pail by turning the axle (instead of by turning the wheel) also did work on the pail. When you turned the axle, you had to apply a much bigger force through a smaller distance. It was a lot easier to lift the pail by turning the wheel. So you see, using a wheel and axle makes a job easier. The machine needs only a small force to lift a heavy object because you apply the force over a large distance.

An Explanation

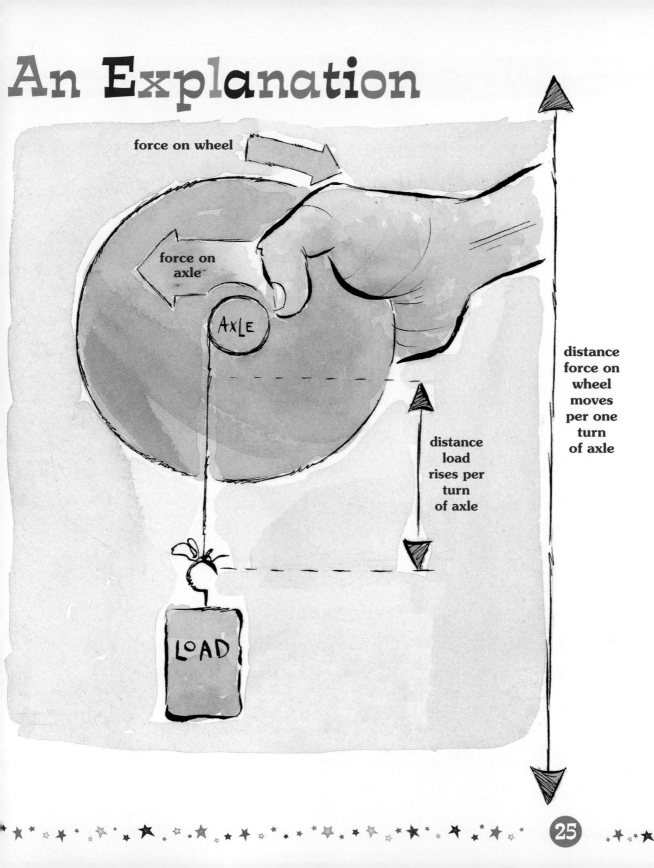

force on wheel

force on axle

AXLE

distance force on wheel moves per one turn of axle

distance load rises per turn of axle

LOAD

6. Wheels, Bearings, and

Early in human history, people learned that moving a load on wheels was easier than sliding (or carrying!) the load. You can see that this is true by doing an experiment.

Let's Begin!

1 Find a wagon. Turn it upside down on level ground.

2 Put several bricks on the wagon. Drag the wagon along the ground for a short distance.

3 Turn the wagon over so that it can roll on its wheels. Put the bricks in the wagon.

4 Pull the wagon along the ground for a short distance.

bricks

bricks

Friction

As you know from Activity 1, friction always goes against motion. Was friction greater when the wagon was on wheels or when it was upside down? Which arrangement required more work to move the wagon the same distance?

There is also friction between a wheel and its axle. To keep this friction small, ball bearings are used.

❺ Place a full one-gallon can on top of an identical can. Notice how hard it is to turn the upper can on the lower can.

❻ Place 6 to 10 marbles (ball bearings) of equal size along the rim of the lower can. Then replace the upper can. Do the bearings make it easier to turn the upper can?

paint cans

no marbles

marbles

Wheels, Bearings, and

Friction always goes against motion. There is friction when one surface moves across another. For example, there is friction between a wagon's rolling wheels and the ground. This friction is called rolling friction. It is usually a small force.

When dragging an upside-down wagon, there is sliding friction between wagon and ground. Sliding friction is a bigger force than rolling friction. Because rolling friction is small, using wheels reduces friction. It was easier to pull the wagon on wheels than it was to drag it over the ground.

rolling friction

sliding friction

Friction: An Explanation

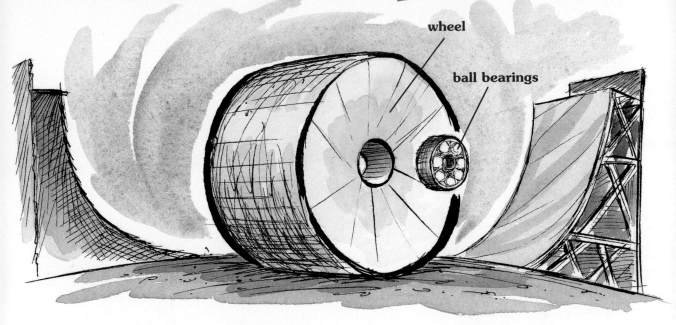

wheel

ball bearings

Usually, wheels turn on an axle. Ball bearings reduce friction between a wheel and its axle. The bearings change sliding friction to rolling friction. So adding ball bearings to wheels makes it even easier to move things.

The harder and smoother the surface of the wheel, and the harder and smoother the surface on which it rolls, the less rolling friction there is. There is little rolling friction between the steel wheels of a train and the steel tracks on which they roll. Wheels rolling on soft ground have to roll uphill. So, a bigger force is needed to keep them rolling.

7. Inclined Planes

 nclined planes (ramps) are everywhere. How do these simple machines make work easier? You can find out!

Let's Begin!

A rubber band can measure force. It stretches when you pull on it (apply a force). The harder the pull, the longer it becomes.

❶ Attach a rubber band to a toy truck. If necessary, tape some weight to the truck. The truck and weight should weigh at least a pound (half a kilogram).

❷ Make an inclined plane. Lean one end of a long board against a chair.

❸ Using the rubber band, pull the truck slowly up the ramp. Have a friend measure the length of the rubber band as you pull the truck.

❹ Without the inclined plane, lift the truck from the floor to the chair. How long is the rubber band now?

❺ How far must you lift the truck to move it from the floor to the chair? How far will it travel if you use the inclined plane to move it from floor to chair?

6 Make the ramp steeper. Predict how this will change the force needed to pull the truck up the ramp.

How does an inclined plane make work easier?

Things you will need:

✔ long, thin rubber band (about 4 to 6 inches x 1/16 inch); several shorter ones can be connected if necessary
✔ large toy truck (at least 6 inches long)
✔ tape
✔ a weight to add to the truck
✔ kitchen or postal scale
✔ board 4 to 5 feet long and wider than the toy truck
✔ chair
✔ a friend
✔ ruler or yardstick

rubber band

yardstick

weight

tape

tape

weight

rubber band

Inclined Planes:

Rolling something up an inclined plane is easier than lifting it straight up to the same height. It takes less force to move the object. The force to roll it up the incline is less than the object's weight, but it has to travel farther. Does that sound familiar? As with other machines, you can use less force over a bigger distance and do the same amount of work.

The drawing shows an inclined plane 2 feet long. It shows a weight that needs to be lifted 1 foot. The length of the incline is twice the height the weight is to be raised. The force to move the weight along the incline is 1 pound. It is half the force needed to lift the weight. The work done (force times distance) is the same either way:

2 pounds × 1 foot (lifted) ≈ 1 pound × 2 feet (moved along the incline)

An Explanation

The force needed will increase if the incline is steeper. But steeper inclines reduce the length traveled. Making the incline longer (less steep) reduces the force needed to move something along it. It is easier to pedal your bike up a gentle slope than up a steep hill.

Inclined planes are common, but very useful. And, like many other simple machines, they make work easier.

8. The Wedge

A wedge is really a double-sided inclined plane. But objects do not move up the wedge. It is the wedge that moves. Wedges can be used to push things apart. You can make a small wedge from a 3-inch x 5-inch file card.

Let's Begin!

Things you will need:
- ✔ 3-inch x 5-inch file card
- ✔ ruler
- ✔ tape
- ✔ cardboard

❶ Fold the file card in half, as shown.

❷ Fold 1/2 inch of each end of the card toward each other, as shown.

❸ Tape these folded ends together. You now have a small wedge.

❹ Use your wedge to lift a piece of cardboard. Slowly push the wedge under the cardboard. Push until you have raised the cardboard as high as possible.

How far did the wedge move as it lifted the cardboard? How far upward did the end of the card-board move? How could you make your wedge stronger? How do you think a wedge makes work easier? Can you think of tools or other devices that are really wedges?

2½"

½"

½"

3"

tape

The Wedge:

edges are inclined planes that move. A wedge moving under or into something creates a force sideways to its motion. An axe is a wedge. When it strikes a log, it pushes the wood apart.

A small force on the wedge you made lifted a heavy piece of cardboard (the load). When you moved the wedge two inches, the cardboard was raised 1/2 inch (the thickness of the wedge). Like other simple machines, a small force on the wedge put a large force on a load. How is this possible? It's the same old story!

An Explanation

The small force moved the wedge two inches. The heavier load (the cardboard) moved only 1/2 inch. Your work on the wedge was about the same as the work done on the cardboard.

$$F \times D \approx F \times D$$

| small force on wedge | large distance force moved | large force to lift cardboard | small distance cardboard was lifted |

Other tools or devices that are wedges or contain wedges include doorstops, chisels, knives, saws, nails, locks and keys, can openers, zippers, and plows.

plow

nail

knife

saw

9. The Screw or Bolt

Screws and bolts are inclined planes wound around a cylinder. To see that this is true, make a very thin inclined plane.

Let's Begin!

1 Cut out a paper triangle 11 inches along the base and 6 inches high.

2 Starting with the wide end, wind the paper around a pencil. The inclined plane is now spiraled around the pencil.

3 Compare what you made with the threads on a bolt or screw.

4 Screws and bolts make work easier. To see how, put a nut on a large, long bolt. Add a wide washer and a plastic bottle with a neck narrower than the washer (see drawing).

5 Place the bottom of the bottle against a heavy object such as a concrete block. Put a marker (an open paper clip will do) at the end of the block. The marker will let you see that the block does move.

6 Put your foot on the end of the bolt so that it cannot move. Use a wrench to turn the nut. The washer will push on the bottle, making the block move.

It is easy to move the block by turning the nut. How hard is it to move the block by hand?

Things you will need:
- ✔ paper
- ✔ ruler
- ✔ scissors
- ✔ pencil
- ✔ large, long bolt and nut
- ✔ wide washer that fits on bolt
- ✔ plastic bottle, such as aspirin bottle, with a neck narrower than the washer, or metal or plastic tube
- ✔ heavy object, such as a concrete block
- ✔ marker, such as an open paper clip
- ✔ wrench to turn the nut

concrete block

nut

washer

plastic bottle or tube

The Screw or Bolt:

The threads of a screw or bolt are a continuous inclined plane. But the threads are very close together. A nut on a bolt moves only from one thread to the next each time it is turned. It moves only a short distance with each turn.

As you found in the section about the wheel and axle, it requires little force to turn the nut with a wrench. Using another machine, the bolt, makes the work even easier. You used a small force to turn the nut around once. But your force (your hand) moved a large distance. The nut put a big force on the block over a very short distance—the distance between one thread and the next.

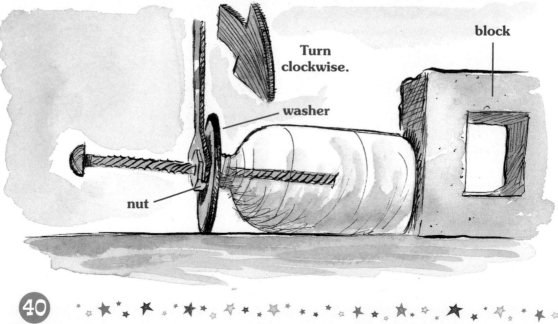

Turn clockwise.

washer

block

nut

An Explanation

The work you did is about the same as the work done on the block:

$$\text{F} \quad \times \quad \textbf{D} \quad \approx \quad \textbf{F} \quad \times \quad \text{D}$$

your small force   **large distance**   **large force on**   **small distance**
on the wrench   **your hand moved**   **the nut**   **the block moved**

You can find the distance the block moved. It is the distance between one thread and the next, multiplied by the number of times the nut was turned.

Other gadgets that use screws or bolts are faucets, vises, and corkscrews.

Idea for Your Science Fair

★ Archimedes made a screw from wood that was used to move water up a hill. See if you can build something similar from plastic tubing, tape, and a coffee can.

10. Single Pulleys

A pulley can be fixed (stay in one place) or it can move. You can experiment with both kinds.

Let's Begin!

❶ **Ask an adult** to use a hook to attach a single pulley to a workbench or beam.

❷ Add about two quarts of water to a plastic pail. Lift the pail with your hands to test its weight.

❸ Tie a strong string to the pail (load). Run the string over the fixed pulley. Pull down on the string to lift the load. Does the pulley make it easier to lift the load? Why or why not?

❹ If you have a spring scale, measure the force needed to raise the load with and without the pulley (see drawing). Does the pulley make work easier?

❺ To attach a movable pulley to the load, tie a string to the hook. Run the string through the pulley. Attach the pail (load) to the pulley. You can now lift the load with the movable pulley. If you have a spring scale, measure the force to raise the load with the movable pulley.

Why might a movable pulley make work easier?

fixed pully

spring scale

load

Things you will need:
- ✔ an adult
- ✔ 1 single pulley (obtain from your school's science room or a hardware store)
- ✔ workbench or beam
- ✔ strong string
- ✔ weight such as a plastic pail with water
- ✔ hooks
- ✔ spring scale (optional)

movable pully

Single Pulleys:

As you may have discovered, it takes more force to lift the load using the fixed pulley than to lift it by hand. The distance the load moves (d) is the same distance you pull the rope (d). Unlike with some simple machines, your force moves the same distance as the load. To do the work needed to lift the load, your force has to be the same as the weight of the load. Actually, your force has to be a bit larger than the load. Why? Because you have to overcome friction in the pulley.

A fixed pulley does not make work easier. So why would anyone use one? The answer is the pulley allows you to change the direction of your force. Pulling down is less likely to strain your back than pulling up.

With the movable pulley, you pulled the string twice as far as the load moved. Both sides of the string had to move as much as the load moved. This should make your force half as big as the weight of the load. But, again, there is friction in the pulley. Your force must be more than half the weight of the load.

An Explanation

fixed pully

d

LOAD

d

movable pully

D

D=2d

LOAD

d

Ideas for Your Science Fair

★ Use two or more pulleys to lift a load. Figure out why multiple pulleys can make work easier.

★ Make some pulleys from ordinary materials you can find.

Words to Know

force—A push or a pull, often measured in pounds or kilograms.

friction—The force that goes against the motion of one object over another.

inclined plane—A simple machine made of a ramp. It reduces the force needed to raise an object to a greater height.

lever—A simple machine made of a rigid bar that can turn on a fixed point called the fulcrum.

load—The object on which a simple machine does work.

pulley—A simple machine consisting of a grooved wheel and a string or rope. It can be used to change the direction of a force.

screw or bolt—A simple machine that is made of a narrow inclined plane wound around a cylinder.

simple machine—A device that makes work easier or changes the direction of a force.

wedge—A simple machine that is made of two inclined planes. It moves under an object to lift it or into other objects to split them apart.

wheel and axle—A simple machine that transfers the work done on the larger wheel to the smaller axle.

work—A force times the distance the force moves as it acts on an object.

Further Reading

Books

Bombaugh, Ruth. *Science Fair Success, Revised and Expanded.* Springfield, N.J.: Enslow Publishers, Inc., 1999.

Farndon, John. *Levers, Wheels, and Pulleys.* Tarrytown, N.Y.: Marshall Cavendish, 2002.

Gardner, Robert. *Heavy-Duty Science Projects With Weight: How Much Does It Weigh?* Berkeley Heights, N.J.: Enslow Publishers, Inc., 2003.

Hodge, Deborah. *Simple Machines.* Buffalo, N.Y.: Kids Can Press, 2000.

Locke, Ian. *The Wheel and How It Changed the World.* New York: Facts on File, Inc., 1995.

Internet Addresses

MIKIDS.com. *Simple Machines.* © 1997-2005. <http://www.mikids.com/Smachines.htm>.

The Museum of Science, Boston. © 1997. *Inventor's Toolbox.* "The Elements of Machines." <http://www.mos.org/sln/Leonardo/Inventors Toolbox.html>.

Index